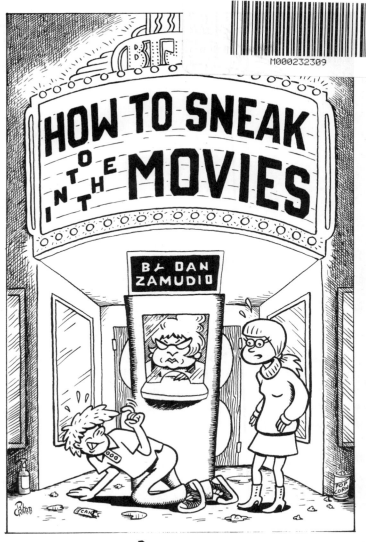

Loompanics Unlimited
Port Townsend, Washington

This book is sold for information purposes only. Neither the author nor the publisher will be held accountable for the use or misuse of the information contained in this book.

HOW TO SNEAK INTO THE MOVIES
© 1995 by Dan Zamudio

Cover and interior illustrations by Robert Crabb

Published by:
Loompanics Unlimited
P.O. Box 1197
Port Townsend, WA 98368

Loompanics Unlimited is a division of Loompanics Enterprises, Inc.

ISBN 1-55950-121-9
Library of Congress Catalog Card Number 94-72981

CONTENTS

ACKNOWLEDGMENTS

This book is dedicated to me, for my hard work and long hours typing, all the money spent on ribbons for my word processor, and all the friends I lost who felt a book about sneaking in would destroy their way of life.

Also dedicated to all the people who think the studios are putting out trash and it's about time for us to fight back.

Special thanks to Ginger McManus (a graduate of Wesleyan University) who spent hours correcting my grammar and punctuation, and who suggested sentences like "The most common problem is the difficulty presented by a confrontation with a potentially overzealous ticket taker who fastidiously adheres to preventative regulations" be included in this book.

INTRODUCTION

The high price that movie theaters charge for a ticket sucks. Each year it seems the price for a ticket increases while the quality of the movies continually decreases. There was a time when I would pay that outrageous ticket price, watch the movie, then leave the theater feeling like I just wasted my money. Each time I paid that $7.50 for a ticket, I was taking a gamble, and usually lost. Going to the movies was no longer fun. I would sit in the theater thinking about the money spent, instead of relaxing and having a good time.

Then one night, after wasting my money on one of those multi-million-dollar-blockbuster movies, I vowed that until the studios started making movies worth spending seven dollars and fifty cents to see, I would never pay full price again. So I began to seek out ways to beat the high cost of movie tickets and still see movies at a theater. I decided to become more selective about what I would see. I even started to listen to the movie critics; that was a mistake. Usually after I saw a movie they recommended, I would leave the theater angry at myself for listening to them and once again wasting my money. Then I thought, "Hey, if the critics get to see the movies for free, why can't I?" And so began my career of sneaking into movies.

The first few times I tried sneaking in I was caught. But each time I was caught, I would retrace my steps and figure out where I went wrong. I started to notice that the more I sneaked in, the easier it became.

Then one day, as I was walking past a movie theater, I noticed some kids hanging out by the exit doors. It was obvious to anyone passing that these kids were going to try to sneak in. I decided to sit down and watch. Finally, the moment they were waiting for came: the doors opened. The group of kids pushed their way past the people exiting, through the doors, and into the theater. For some reason I had a feeling that it wouldn't be long before I would see those kids again, so I remained seated. Well, not more than a minute later, the doors opened and out they came followed by several employees of the theater. I laughed to myself and thought, "Those fools. With all the mistakes they were making I'm surprised they weren't caught sooner. Man, someone should write a book on how to sneak into movies without being caught. Hey, why not me?"

I thought it was a fun idea so I mentioned it to a few friends. I was surprised to find how seriously they disapproved of the idea. Their common criticism was that they feared that theater security would be tightened and it might even "put an end to sneaking in."

For awhile I agreed with them, but then I thought, "The people who run the theaters already know how people sneak in. I'm not telling them anything new. Plus, the owners will be relying on their employees to take the time out of their busy schedules to actually read this book. Fact: Most theater employees would rather sit down and watch a two hour movie version of a book instead of taking a week to read it."

So, with that in mind, I started to write. I want to clarify that I did not write this book with the intent that it would be used as a criminal guide for juvenile delinquents. Instead, I wrote it as a way to fight back against the studios for the trash they continually release and expect us to accept. Until the studios start making movies worth that high ticket price, there's no reason anyone should pay it. So, in addition to sneaking in, I have also included a few chapters on other ways to beat the high cost of movie tickets, ways to get the ticket for as little as a dollar or even to be paid to go to the movies. So have fun, save money, and keep in mind that sneaking in is "sort of" illegal... so be smart.

There are many ways to beat the high cost of movie tickets. The most common are:

1. Sneaking in
2. Matinee and Twilight Screenings
3. Second-run Theaters (Dollar Houses)
4. Renting A Video

All of these ways (except Renting A Video) offer you the opportunity to see movies at a theater, without paying full price. Once you have become fully aware of the many different, easy ways to beat the high cost of movie tickets, you will wonder why you ever paid full price.

Throughout this book, I will illustrate the ideas using real-life examples of how to sneak into the movies. These "case histories" are based on theaters in Chicago and Los Angeles, where I have had the most experience. I'll tell you the security strengths and weaknesses for each of these theaters, any special tips, and rate each one on a Degree of Difficulty scale from one ★ (the easiest) to five ★★★★★ (the hardest). An example is shown below.

I'm not encouraging you to sneak into these theaters. I'm just trying to show you how every theater has its own peculiar features which make it easy or hard to sneak in. These sidebars are meant to stimulate your thinking about how to apply the ideas in my book.

Chicago, Illinois
Degree of Difficulty: 1 ★

This theater is a dream come true for those who sneak in. It has many auditoriums showing many different movies and is always crowded. Best of all, every method works there. The auditoriums are all located down one long hallway. At the front of the hallway is a giant lobby which separates the ticket taker from the concession stand. This huge lobby makes it easy to blend in with the crowds. An easy way to enter the theater is to use the door that connects the parking structure to the lobby. People are always going in and out of the door, so it's simple to walk through and blend with the crowds. The only problem is that this door is located next to the ticket taker. On weekends, the ticket taker is too busy ripping tickets to keep a constant eye on the door, so you shouldn't worry. One other thing to be aware of is that there are many security cameras located throughout the theater. It is nearly impossible for anyone watching the monitors to notice you sneaking around unless you are completely obvious. Be smart.

SNEAKING IN

The number one way to beat the high cost of movies tickets and still see first run movies at a theater, is to sneak in. There are four basic methods that can be used to sneak in. They are:

1. Pay For One, Stay For More
2. Desperate Emergency Approach (Bathroom Trick)
3. In Thru The Out Door
4. Blend In With Crowd (Adopt A Family)

Each method has about a hundred variations. But no matter which variation you use, it should still follow the same structure as the method from which it was derived. Determining which method to use will depend on many factors, such as the time of day, the amount of people at the theater, and the method you are most comfortable using.

In order to become really good at sneaking in you must first overcome the fear of doing it. The number one fear which prevents people from sneaking in is the Fear Of Being Caught. I will cover What Happens And What To Do When Caught later in the book. Once you overcome that fear, going to the movies will never be the same again.

Things To Do Before Sneaking In

Before attempting to sneak in, there are a few things you must do. The first and most important is to make a list or schedule of the movies you want to see. In order to make this list you must do a little research at home with the local newspaper movie listings. Using the movie listings, find the theater that is playing the most movies that you are interested in seeing. The larger the theater, the better the chances are of sneaking in and possibly seeing more than one movie. The movie listings will let you know the movies that are playing at each theater, the time the movie begins, and the phone number of the theater. Now, call the theater. Usually when you call the number in the paper, you will get a recorded message of the movies and their start times. Double check the start times in the paper with the start times on the message. At the end of the message there will be an additional "for more information" number. Write it down. This number will connect you with a theater employee. Call and ask the employee what the running times are for the movies you are interested in seeing. The running time is the exact length of the film from the minute it begins to the final credits. Once you have that information, you will be able to make your schedule.

Often, the reason people are caught when trying to sneak in is that they have no idea which movies are ending and which are about to begin. They will bring unwanted attention to themselves by walking in and out of auditoriums that have movies already in progress, hoping to find a movie that is about to start. Having a schedule will help prevent you from making that mistake.

The schedule will list the movies you want to see and the order in which to see them. Having both the start times and the running times, your list will be a down-to-the-minute accurate schedule of where, in the theater, it's safe to be. The schedule should be planned so that when one movie ends, the next on the list is just about ready to begin. The less time between movies, the easier it will be to blend in with the crowds entering the different auditoriums. Anything more than fifteen minutes between each movie will increase your chances of being caught. Having a precise schedule will help raise your awareness of what's going on around you, build your confidence, and increase your chances of a successful sneak-in. If you feel a schedule is unnecessary, attempt sneaking in a few times without it, then try using it one time. You will definitely notice a difference.

Before I went to the theater on one occasion, I decided to call and double check on the start times. It was a good thing that I did because I found out that at eight p.m. that evening the theater was having an "advance screening" of a movie I had been eagerly waiting to see. I then called the "for more information" number to find out the running time of that screening. I had intended to go to the twilight screening that night, so I worked out a plan to see a movie that would end just before the "advance screening" would begin. Plus, I selected an alternate movie that started around eight, in case I couldn't get into the screening. Well, that night I not only saw the twilight movie and the "advance screening," I also saw a third movie that played after the "advance screening" in the same auditorium. Not a bad evening for only three dollars and fifty cents.

Waukegan, Illinois

Degree of Difficulty: 2 ★★

This is the theater where sneaking in was perfected. It has two sections: one section has four auditoriums, the other has eight. There is one ticket taker at the front of each section. As you enter the theater's lobby area, check which side is showing the movie you want to see. Then use any sneaking-in method to get past the ticket takers. There is no way to get from one section to the other, so try to pick the section that has the most movies you want to see playing in it.

Pay For One, Stay For More

This is the most basic and easiest of the sneaking in methods. This method, and all other sneaking in methods in this book, is most effective at theaters that are multi-plexes. Multi-plexes are the theaters with more than four auditoriums. That doesn't mean that sneaking in won't work at theaters with only one or two auditoriums, but it will be more difficult. This method is easy to do strictly because you actually pay to get into the theater. Remember, if you choose to pay, NEVER PAY FULL PRICE. Only pay a Matinee or Twilight Screening ticket price, topics which I will cover later in this book.

What To Do

If done correctly, the Pay For One, Stay For More method will almost never fail. Here's how it's done: after the movie you paid to see has ended, remain in your seat and watch the credits. At this time, the theater employees are usually standing outside the auditorium to clean it. After the credits have finished and the lights have come on, the employees waiting to clean will enter the auditorium and get to work. The employees directing people to the exit doors will move on to other things. So, anyone who remained watching the credits can walk out of the auditorium without being noticed by any lobby employees.

Casually leave the auditorium and go directly to the bathroom. While in the bathroom, check your schedule and make the necessary changes in your appearance. Later on in the book I will explain the importance of the bathroom and how to use it to your advantage. Now, wait until a group of people begin to leave the bathroom and blend in with them. Walk out of the bathroom and go directly to the auditorium that is playing the next movie on your list. On your way, pick up a "Movie Facts" or any other free reading material. Enter the auditorium, find a seat, and read or pretend to be asleep; that decision will be made according to the amount of people in the auditorium. If there are not many people in the auditorium, you may become nervous and begin to fear being caught. Pretending to be asleep will help relax you. Plus, the time before the lights go down and the movie begins will seem to pass more quickly. If the auditorium is crowded, feel confident that no employees have noticed you and your safety is assured. Just relax, find a seat, read, and wait for the lights to dim. Once the lights are off and the previews have begun, that will be your sign that you have achieved a successful sneak-in.

Advantages

There are many factors that work to your advantage when using this method, the greatest being that you are in the theater legally. You have actually bought a ticket and will definitely see a movie. Of course, you have only paid to see a matinee or twilight screening, which means that even if you're caught trying to sneak into more movies, you have seen at least one movie at a discounted price.

Chicago, Illinois
Degree of Difficulty: 3 ★★★

This theater is multi-leveled. On the ground level is the box office and ticket taker; the auditoriums are on the other levels. Once you make it past the ticket taker, the chances of being caught are slim. Occasionally, the "Desperate Emergency Approach" will work, but it's best to "Pay For One, Stay For More." This is a nice theater which never has large crowds.

Another factor is the level of chaos within the lobby of the theater between showings. The employees are busy directing people to the exit doors, ripping tickets, cleaning the auditoriums, and tending to the concession stand. It is nearly impossible for the employees to keep track of who is coming to see a movie or who just saw one. It then becomes easy for anyone to blend in with the crowds that are walking into the different auditoriums. Never wear something that may be easy to remember or would make you look obviously out of place. Keep in mind that your goal is to be as inconspicuous as possible, so wearing things like bright clothes, jackets with team logos, etc., could lessen your chances of a successful sneak-in.

Another advantage is that the later it gets in the evening, the easier it becomes to sneak around to more movies. Later in the evening, the managers are usually in the offices doing paper work, there are fewer employees working, and the employees that are still there are getting tired and are more concerned about going home than catching people sneaking in. So if you notice an opportunity to see a third movie, go see it. There are not many people that can handle three movies in one day, but if you have nothing else to do, this is a great way to get your money's worth.

Disadvantages

The fact that you actually paid to get into the theater is the only real disadvantage. There's always the chance that the movie you paid to see will suck and that you will get caught trying to sneak into more movies. Never get discouraged about being caught. Use it as a learning experience. The more you learn about the theater and the employees' routines, the better your chances are of sneaking around the next time.

Problems You Might Encounter

Even though all theaters are run differently, they do share some of the same methods of stopping people from sneaking around to different auditoriums. The most common problem, or inconvenience, is the Employee At The Auditorium Doors. This is the method in which an employee is standing outside the auditorium doors checking ticket stubs before letting the people in to see the movie. When you notice that happening, either buy or try to find some popcorn or a drink. That popcorn or drink will become a "prop." Now, with your prop in hand, approach the employee that is checking the stubs and say, "My girlfriend has the stubs — I just had to go buy her some popcorn."

It's a fact: anytime a guy takes a girl to the movies, sometime before or during the movie he will be sent to get her some popcorn, or a drink, or Twizzlers, or a napkin, or mustard, or a pretzel, or anything that will keep him from sitting in his seat and relaxing. Most often, the employee checking the stubs is a guy; therefore, he will be able to relate to your story and will let you into the auditorium. If you are a girl, just walk up to the employee and say, "I was already in." Theater employees are always trying to "pick up on" the girls and never want to give a bad impression of themselves. They will never second guess anything a girl says.

Chicago, Illinois
Degree of Difficulty: 2 ★★

Like the last theater, this is also multi-leveled. The only difference is that this is bigger and attracts more people. This is a fun, easy theater to spend the whole day in.

Another way to get past the employee at the auditorium door is to wait until he leaves and a new employee takes his place. Many times the first employee has stepped away to take care of some personal business and will only be gone for a couple of minutes, so you have to act quickly. Approach the new employee and say, "I was already in. The guy that was here before, the one with the blond hair, said I could get back in." Always give a small description of the first employee. It will help to make your story more authentic and believable. Then walk past the employee and find a seat.

Most of the smaller auditoriums have only one entrance where the employee checking ticket stubs is standing. But if the auditorium is big, it will have several entrance doors and, quite often, will still have only one employee checking the stubs. It's always best to find a way of getting into the auditorium without approaching the employee. Usually there will be one door open, where the employee will be standing; the other doors will be closed. At times the closed doors will be opened by some guy coming out of the auditorium to get something for his date. When you notice the doors open, make sure that the employee is busy checking stubs, then walk in the auditorium before the door closes. Many times the employee will see you go in, but he will be too busy to stop you or will assume he has already checked your ticket. Relax, find a seat, and wait for the movie to begin.

If you find you have to leave the auditorium for any reason, approach the employee checking the stubs and say, "I left my ticket in my jacket. I just want to be sure I can get back in without it." Since the employee does see you in the auditorium, he will assume you really do have a ticket and will say it's okay. Once you're in the auditorium, it's usually a good idea to stay in. There's no reason you should risk the chance of not being able to get back in.

Advice

The best advice is always to make the first movie you see the movie you want to see. This holds true for all the sneaking-in methods. There's always the chance you might not be able to sneak around the theater. So if you paid, make it worth your money.

If you ever feel that the employees are watching and the chances of being caught are too great, just give up and leave the theater. It's always best to leave the theater on your own, without being escorted by employees. Remember, you did see one movie at a discounted price, and that's good.

Burbank, California
Degree of Difficulty: 3 ★★★ (Sneaking in without paying)
1 ★ (Pay for one, Stay for more)

Fun big theater with many screens. Always packed on weekends. Any sneaking in method will work, but it is incredibly easy to "Pay For One, Stay For More." Be aware that some of the employees carry "walkie-talkies." So, be extra careful when sneaking in without paying.

Since you are in the theater legally, take some time to walk around. Learn the employees' favorite hang-out spots, location of the unguarded doors, and anything else that may help you sneak around in the future.

And last, always remember that having some popcorn or a drink in hand will help to create the illusion of having recently arrived at the theater. If an employee ever asks to see a ticket stub, just say, "I think I forgot it at the concession stand." The employee will see the popcorn and drink and believe your story.

As mentioned before, the PAY FOR ONE, STAY FOR MORE method is the easiest and most basic method, primarily due to the fact that you paid to get into the theater. The last three methods, THE DESPERATE EMERGENCY APPROACH (BATHROOM TRICK), IN THRU THE OUT DOOR, and BLEND IN WITH THE CROWD (ADOPT A FAMILY) all consist of sneaking into the theater without paying anything. If you found PAY FOR ONE, STAY FOR MORE a little too risky, feel free to skip over the next few methods and go right to the WHAT HAPPENS AND WHAT TO DO WHEN CAUGHT chapter. But if you like a challenge, like to live on the edge, then the fun is about to begin.

The following methods are going to sound almost too easy to actually work. But they do work, almost every time. Keep in mind that even the simplest things can be done incorrectly. The primary reason people are caught when trying to sneak in is that they make dumb little mistakes. If you follow the structure of these methods, you should be able to avoid making those mistakes and greatly increase your chances of successfully sneaking into the movies.

One last note: these methods work best when you are alone. Once mastered, these methods will allow you to sneak others in as well. The chapter HOW TO SNEAK IN WITH MORE THAN ONE PERSON will give you some ideas on how to do that. Until then, let's focus on the basics.

The Desperate Emergency Approach (Bathroom Trick)

Out of all the sneaking-in methods, this is the only method in which you will actually have to approach an employee in order to sneak in. The effectiveness of this method depends on two factors:

1. Your acting ability
2. The mood of the ticket taker.

This method works best when the ticket taker is overwhelmed with people waiting to get into the theater. This will actually occur on Friday or Saturday night. At that time the ticket taker's main concern is to rip tickets and let people in as quickly as possible. Occasionally, the Desperate Emergency Approach will work when the theater is not busy, but the chances of being caught are greater.

What To Do

The first thing you must do is come up with some sort of desperate emergency story to tell the ticket taker. This is the point when your acting skills will play a crucial part. Some examples of stories that have been known to work are:

1. "Is there any way I can use your phone? My car won't start and I need to call for help."
2. "I just came out of (name a movie that just ended) and I think I left my keys in there."
3. "Is there any way I can use your bathroom? My friend will be here in a second with the tickets."

Of course, any story that sounds like a really serious emergency will work. For the sake of example, let's focus on the "is there any way I can use your bathroom" story. Before approaching the ticket taker, take a few minutes to organize the details of the story in your mind, and, as they say in acting class, get "in the moment." Once you're "in the moment," all the fear and anxiety you felt about sneaking in will be replaced with the reality of the story. If you have decided to use the bathroom story, there is a great chance that by the time you reach the ticket taker you really will have to use it. That's when you know you're truly "in the moment."

Once you have become "in the moment," approach the ticker taker. Remember, it's very important to remain "in the moment" the whole time, including the time before you reach any employees. Those few seconds before you say anything will play an important part in your success; your body language will be one of the factors used to convince the ticket taker that your story may be a real emergency. Never overact. Always be as natural as possible. If you overdo it, the ticket taker will see right through your story.

Once you reach the ticket taker, in your best desperate-emergency voice, begin your story. This is when the mood of the ticket taker will play a crucial part. If the ticket taker is having a good day, your chances of getting in without any problems are great. But if the ticket taker is having a bad day, your chances are slim. The ticket taker will ask a lot of questions and in the end deny you entrance. If that happens, get a good look at the ticket taker and walk away. Always try to make a mental note about this employee. Knowing which employees to avoid will greatly increase your chances of successfully sneaking in the next time.

Most of the time the ticket taker will let you in without any questions or problems. Once the "go ahead" is given, be sure to ask the ticket taker where the bathroom is located. Asking where the bathroom, phone, etc., is located will give the impression that you have never been to this theater before and that you are only there because it was the nearest place to go for help. If you go directly to the bathroom without asking directions, it may cause the ticket taker to become suspicious. If that happens, another employee may be asked to keep an eye on you and all your plans will be ruined. There are always those employ-ees that are trying to win "Employee of the Month" or get promoted up to manager and will do things like that. Always follow through with whatever story you choose, then somehow find your way into the bath-room. For example, if you asked to use the phone, go and pretend to use it, then hang up and enter the bathroom. In order to successfully sneak in using any method, you must always find a way of ending up in the bathroom.

The bathroom is the safest place to be and will play an important part of sneaking in successfully. Three key things take place in the bathroom that will work to your advantage:

1. Stalling for time
2. Metamorphosis
3. Blending in with the crowd

Stalling for Time. After you have entered the bath-room, go directly to a stall and close the door. This will give you a chance to "stall for time." If an em-ployee has been following you, he will usually give up his pursuit the moment you close the stall door. Sometimes the employee may stay in the bathroom for several minutes, combing his hair or washing his hands, trying to act like he's not following you. After a while the employee will get bored and leave. The longer you stay in the stall, the better the chances are that the employee will forget about you. One of the most common mistakes people make in the bath-room is that of passing time by fixing their hair or standing around looking confused. Entering a stall will keep you concealed and give you plenty of time to concentrate on the next thing, metamorphosis.

Metamorphosis. "Metamorphosis" means "a complete change of form, structure, or appearance." Theater employees see hundreds of people per day. It's nearly impossible for them to remember what every single person looks like. At the most, the employee might remember a shirt, a hat, or even a hair style. To change your appearance slightly will transform you into a whole new person in the eyes of the employee. While in the stall, make the necessary changes: put on a hat, take off a jacket, do anything that will make your appearance different. With proper scheduling, by the time the "metamorphosis" is complete, a movie has ended and people are beginning to fill the bathroom. When you begin to hear people entering the bathroom, finish the metamorphosis, flush the toilet, and prepare to blend in with the crowd.

Blend In With The Crowd. When you notice a line forming outside the stall door, come out of the stall and do anything you might naturally do: wash your hands, fix your hair, tuck in your shirt, etc. This will give you time to check whether or not any employees are still following you. When you feel that everything is safe, casually blend in with the group that is leaving the bathroom and enter the lobby. At this time, the lobby will be chaotic, so it should be easy to avoid being noticed by the ticket taker. It's a good idea to know which auditorium is showing the movie you want to see before you enter the bathroom. This will improve your chances of quickly blending in with the right crowds and avoiding looking around lost and confused.

Advantages
The greatest advantage to using this method (and all the following methods) is that you pay absolutely

nothing to see first-run movies in a theater. If you combine this method with the last part of "Pay For One, Stay For More," it is possible to spend the whole day at the movies for free.

Disadvantages

The biggest disadvantage to using this method is that you depend upon the ticket taker's approval before entering the theater. If the ticket taker denies you entrance, then your plans of seeing a movie at that theater are ruined. Since contact has been made with an employee, it would not be a good idea to try using any other sneaking-in method to get in. There's always the chance that the ticket taker may see you walking around inside the theater, remember refusing you entrance, then have someone throw you out. As odd as it may seem, ticket takers will see hundreds of people a day but will always seem to remember the few to whom they deny entrance. Even resorting to buying a ticket is a bad idea. Buying a ticket will only prove to the ticket taker what he already suspected, that you were trying to sneak in. That will then give him the satisfaction of knowing he outsmarted you, and there's nothing worse than being outsmarted by a ticket taker.

Problems You Might Encounter

The most common problem is "The Ticket Taker That Likes To Make Things Difficult." Before letting you in, the ticket taker may ask you to:

1. put your name on a list the theater uses to keep track of the people that enter without a ticket
2. leave some identification with him.

Both of these minor difficulties can be overcome with a little creativity.

If the ticket taker wants you to put your name on a list, NEVER WRITE YOUR REAL NAME. It is always best to make up a name, use a friend's name, or use a celebrity's name; any name will work. If you use a famous person's name, choose someone the ticket taker probably wouldn't recognize and always use the less formal version. For instance, instead of writing "Frank Lloyd Wright," write "Frank Wright." After you sign in, the ticket taker will write the time you entered the theater, then leave space to put an out time. Don't worry about that. After about ten minutes the ticker taker will assume you exited a different door, fill in the out time, and forget about you.

Chicago, Illinois
Degree of Difficulty: 3 ★★★

This theater has four auditoriums, three on one side and one in a section by itself. If you decide to sneak in here, focus on the side with three auditoriums. The chances of getting into the one separate auditorium are slim. The best way to get into that auditorium is by finding the one door that connects it to the others. This door is hooked up to an alarm system that is activated every time it is opened. It's not even worth your effort. In the section with three auditoriums, the bathrooms are located on the lower level. There are two sets of stairs leading down to them. One is located by the concession stand and the ticket taker; the other by a door that leads into the larger of the three auditoriums. This can help when sneaking from the two smaller auditoriums into the larger one. The best way to get in without paying is to have a receipt from the cafe, which is also located in the Fine Arts Building. The cafe does not have a bathroom, so their customers are allowed to use the theater's, but only if they show proof (the receipt). This theater focuses mostly on foreign films, films by independents, and films that don't appeal to mainstream audiences.

If the ticket taker wants you to leave identification, just say, "My wallet was stolen the other day and all my I.D. was in it." You never want to leave any form of identification, not even an old I.D. Leaving any picture I.D. will help the ticket taker remember what you looked like and make it easier to find you. After you tell the ticket taker you don't have I.D., say, "Listen, how about if I just leave my keys. That way you know I'll be right back. I can't leave without them." Remember, you're "in the moment" and experiencing a desperate emergency. You need to get into the theater to use the phone or bathroom. The ticket taker will then say, "All right, just leave your keys and come right back." Any time you plan to sneak in using this method, it's always a good idea to bring along a set of old keys. This will be a great way to get rid of them. Give the keys to the ticket taker, enter the theater, and never come back. Later that evening, the ticket taker will put the keys in the lost-and-found and forget about you.

Advice

The most important advice is always to stick to one story. Pick one desperate emergency and stay with it until the end. Even if you are denied entrance, remain "in the moment" until you are out of viewing distance of the ticket taker.

When in the bathroom stall, try not to spend too much time inside. If you stay too long, someone waiting to use it may become concerned about you and start asking if you're okay. You never want to attract attention to yourself in any way. Remember, your goal is to blend in without being noticed by anyone, including those people who actually paid for a ticket. People who paid don't like those who sneak in. Quite often, when they notice someone attempting to sneak in, they will inform an employee and ruin all plans.

One Friday night, I was looking through the L.A. Weekly for something to do. I noticed that the Chinese Theater was showing a couple of movies I wanted to see, so I decided to try to sneak in there. I called the theater to find out the running times and noticed that both movies would be ending around the same time. I also found out that one movie was playing in the main auditorium, the other in the side auditorium.

Chicago, Illinois
Degree of Difficulty: 3 ★★★

There are three auditoriums at this theater; two smaller auditoriums on the ground level and one big auditorium downstairs. To sneak from a ground level auditorium to the one downstairs is easy, but to sneak from downstairs up is slightly more difficult. The bathrooms are located on the downstairs level. This is helpful when sneaking in using any method. There are two sets of stairs, one at each end of the theater. The entrance and the ticket taker are always set up at one of the stairways. The other stairway will have an employee posted next to it only when the movie playing at the downstairs level has ended. The employee will be there to direct people out of the theater and to prevent them from sneaking into the other two auditoriums. Call the theater first and find out which auditorium is showing the movie you want to see. This will help you decide which method to use and will increase your chances for a successful sneak in.

When I arrived at the theater, I noticed the ticket taker at the main auditorium was busy with a crowd of people trying to get in. When I reached the ticket taker I asked him if I could use the bathroom. He said I should go to the other entrance and the ticket taker there would let me in. Even though I knew where the other entrance was, I still asked how to get to it. When I got there the ticket taker was half asleep. I told him the guy at the other door said I could use the bathroom. He hardly looked at me, then waved me in. When I came out of the bathroom, the lobby was packed. So I blended in with the crowd and walked into the auditorium that was playing one of the movies I came to see. That was probably one of the easiest times I ever sneaked in.

A friend and I had just finished a long day of work and were walking to our cars when we decided to stop at a theater to use the bathroom. This was before the City Walk was built, so the only bathrooms in the area were inside the theater. We were both really tired and the thought of sneaking in wasn't even on our minds. When we reached the ticket taker, we told him how we had just got off of work and needed to use the bathroom before the long drive home. My friend and I both had bags of clothes with us, which helped to prove that our story was true. He then asked us to leave some I.D. or keys with him. I said I didn't have any I.D. with me. My friend said she had keys but they were in the bottom of her bag. She then started to go through her bag in search of them. A line began to form behind us. Finally the ticket taker became frustrated and said, "All right, just go in."

After we came out of the bathroom, my friend turned to me and said, "You know, we could probably stay and see a movie if we wanted." Neither of us had plans that evening, so we decided to stay. We looked out of place carrying bags of clothes and knew we had to find an auditorium quickly. We noticed people entering an auditorium, found a seat in the back, hid our bags, and waited. A few minutes later the lights went down. When the movie ended, we exited the back doors. On the way to our cars, my friend told me that was the first time she had ever sneaked in and she couldn't believe how easy it was.

In Thru The Out Door

When someone mentions the idea of sneaking into the movies, this is usually the first method that comes to most people's minds. It is the most common and probably the oldest method used for sneaking in anywhere. But, because this method is so popular, most people believe they automatically know how to do it correctly. Remember, even the simplest things can be done wrong. When using this method, you can:

1. arrive at the theater without a plan and take your chances, or
2. arrive at the theater with a down-to-the-minute plan and greatly increase your chances of success.

This method is most effective when large crowds of people are exiting the theater after a movie has ended. After a film ends, many people will exit the theater using back doors and doors not commonly used. In a theater showing several popular new releases, people will be exiting many different doors, and this will offer the best opportunity for a successful sneak in.

What To Do

The first and most important thing to do is to call the theater and find out the running times of the movies you want to see. This will play a major part in the success of this method. Having the running times will allow you to approximate what time people will begin exiting the theater and when you should arrive.

The best time to arrive is about ten minutes before the movie ends. This will allow you plenty of time to walk around the outside of the theater to find a door out of viewing distance of any employee.

Choosing a door in the back of the theater is always the best bet. These doors are usually unguarded by employees and will often lead directly into an auditorium. The problem with using the back doors is that very few people exit them, so timing and speed are very important. After you find a door, DO NOT STAND RIGHT NEXT TO IT — always stand a small distance away. The most common mistake people make is to stand next to the exit door, waiting for someone to open it. Standing right next to the door will only:

1. announce to the world that you're planning to sneak in
2. increase your chances of being noticed by an employee, security guard, or people on their way to buy a ticket.

Your goal is to be standing just far enough from the door so that you can casually walk over and grab it as it is closing, without bringing any attention to yourself. Once you grab the door, hold it until it almost closes. Never pull open the door and immediately walk into the theater. You can never be sure whether or not an employee is inside guarding the door. A good way to test for an employee is to hold the door until it almost closes. If you feel someone from inside of the theater pulling the door closed, you will know it is guarded and you will need a new plan. If the door remains open, that will be your sign that it's safe to proceed. If the door you enter leads into a hallway instead of an auditorium, blend in with the crowds and proceed into the bathroom. What to do if the door leads directly into an auditorium will be covered in the ADVANTAGES section.

Often, you may find that the only doors to use will be at the front of the theater. This will make things a bit more challenging. You will now have to find a way to avoid being noticed by any employees working in the front of the theater and still be within distance of the exit doors. The best places to wait are at the side of the theater or across the street. When people begin to exit, casually walk over to the doors. Be sure to keep an eye on all employees within viewing distance. The moment you notice that all employees are busy, squeeze past the people exiting and enter the theater. This time, instead of heading to the bathroom, go directly into the auditorium of whatever film just ended. This is just a precaution, in case any employees have seen you sneak in. If an employee stops you as you're entering just say, "I just got out of (name of the movie that recently ended) and I can't find my keys." Always be aware of which movie has ended. It will help to get you out of uncomfortable situations with employees.

Los Angeles, California
Degree of Difficulty: 2 ★★

The best method to use at this theater is the "In Thru The Out Door." This theater has only one auditorium and will usually only show the big blockbuster movies. There are many exit doors around the theater so the chances of getting in are great. Make sure to call the theater and find out the ending time of the movie. By the time you arrive, people should be exiting the theater. The credits will still be rolling when you enter. So find a seat and wait for the next showing to begin.

Advantages

When using this method, the greatest advantage you hope for is to enter the theater through a door that leads directly into an auditorium where a film is ending. Entering when the auditorium is dark and the credits are still rolling offers you two possibilities:

1. remaining in the auditorium and watching the next showing of that movie, or
2. waiting for the credits to end, then leaving that auditorium and seeing a different movie.

If you choose to stay in the auditorium, find a seat and relax. When the lights come on, the employees will begin cleaning the auditorium. It's possible you may be the only person still in the auditorium besides the employees. Don't worry about that. When you notice an employee approaching the area where you are sitting, politely say to him, "Excuse me, I came a little late and missed the beginning. Is it all right if I stay to see what I missed?" The employee may then ask to see your ticket stub. Since you don't have one, it's best to say, "I was just looking for it. I was in such a hurry to get here that I must have dropped it on the way." Since the employee does see you sitting in the auditorium as the movie is ending, he will assume your story is true and let you stay. Now, if any other employees question you, all you have to say is, "The employee over there knows I was already in." That employee will then go and verify your story. Once your story is confirmed, the employees will finish cleaning and leave the auditorium. A few minutes later, the people who paid for a ticket will begin to enter. That will be the sign of a successful sneak-in.

If you enter the auditorium but decide that you want to see a different movie, just follow the structure of the "Pay For One, Stay For More" method. If you find that the movie you came to see is playing in an auditorium that is too difficult to reach, look around and note what films are showing near you. Then check your schedule for the start times of these movies. If a movie is beginning within ten to fifteen minutes, and you are interested in seeing it, go to that auditorium. But if you find that there is a great amount of time before any of those movies begin, go back to your original auditorium. When the movie in that auditorium begins, watch a bit of it to pass some time, then leave and go directly to the auditorium that is showing the movie you want to see.

Disadvantages

The major disadvantage is the possibility that the only doors to use are at the front of the theater. Since the front of the theater is the area where the majority of employees work, the chances of someone noticing you are greatly increased. Many times, when using the front doors, people will bring unwanted attention to themselves by trying to push their way past the large crowd exiting. If you must use the front doors, always let the crowd thin out a little before trying to sneak in. This will make it easier for you to pass through the doors without bringing attention to yourself.

Problems You Might Encounter

The most common problem you may encounter is the "Employee At The Exit Doors." The theater owners realize that this is the most popular method used for sneaking in. In order to fight back, the owners will place employees at the main exit doors when a film ends. This helps to direct people out of the theater, stops people from sneaking into more movies, and keeps people from coming "In Thru The Out Door."

The only way to know if a theater has employees guarding these doors is to have been in the theater before. This is why it is very important to note how many employees run the theaters every time you're inside.

Chicago, Illinois
Degree of Difficulty: 1 ★

This theater is a dream come true for those who sneak in. It has many auditoriums showing many different movies and is always crowded. Best of all, every method works there. The auditoriums are all located down one long hallway. At the front of the hallway is a giant lobby which separates the ticket taker from the concession stand. This huge lobby makes it easy to blend in with the crowds. An easy way to enter the theater is to use the door that connects the parking structure to the lobby. People are always going in and out of that door, so it's simple to walk through and blend with the crowds. The only problem is that this door is located next to the ticket taker. On weekends, the ticket taker is too busy ripping tickets to keep a constant eye on the door, so you shouldn't worry. One other thing to be aware of is that there are many security cameras located throughout the theater. It is nearly impossible for anyone watching the monitors to notice you sneaking around unless you are completely obvious. Be smart.

Another problem is the "Helpful Employee." If an employee has seen you sneaking in and you've used the "I can't find my keys" story, often that employee will volunteer his services to help you find them. The employee will then walk with you to the auditorium and ask a lot of questions, such as, "Where were you sitting?", "What does the key chain look like?", "Are you sure you had them with you?" After a few minutes of looking around, you should pretend to find them. Then the employee will escort you to the exit doors and ruin all plans of sneaking in.

Not all of the problems you may encounter will be caused by an employee. Many times, the people exiting the back doors will notice you on your way to grab the door. Those people will then purposefully close the door before you reach it. If that happens you can either find another door or wait at the original door and hope someone else will be exiting. But, for the most part, your plans of using this method to sneak in may be temporarily ruined.

Advice

If you ever enter through an out door and immediately encounter an employee, look at him and smile, then turn around and walk out. At that point both you and the employee know what is going on and there is no use in trying to make up a story. Never get discouraged when something like that happens. See the humor in the situation and remember never to use that door again.

Blend In With Crowd
(Adopt A Family)

Of all the sneaking in methods in this book, the "Blend In With Crowd" is the most challenging. Even though the possibility of success is slim and depends on a great deal of luck, there are times when it can be used effectively. This method works best on opening nights when groups of friends and families are likely to go to the movies. The effectiveness of this method depends on how well you are able to blend in with the group of friends and family, without anyone suspecting you don't belong.

What To Do

Your primary focus from the moment you arrive at the theater is to observe whether or not the ticket taker is counting every ticket when large groups approach him. Many times, when a large group or family approach the ticket taker, one person in the group will hand all the tickets to the employee. The ticket taker will take the stack of tickets, rip them all at once without counting them, then give the stubs to that person. He will then let anyone that looks like they belong to the group into the theater, assuming that everyone had bought a ticket. Your goal is to become part of that group.

First, find a safe place outside the theater to wait for a group of friends or family to arrive that you feel will be easy to blend in with. When you find a group about to enter the theater and one person is holding all the tickets, casually walk over and join them. Try to stand close enough to the group to look like you are part of it, without being noticed by any of the group's members. Be sure to keep an eye on the ticket taker when the tickets are handed to him. If he counts the tickets, quickly make up a "Desperate Emergency" story and get "in the moment." But, if he rips the tickets without counting them, walk past the ticket taker with the group and enter the theater. Hang around the group for a few minutes, then separate yourself and find the bathroom. In the bathroom, make the necessary changes, then go to the movie you came to see.

Advantages

The number one advantage is the "Ticket Taker Who Never Counts The Tickets." Usually the ticket taker will start the day counting tickets, but if large groups continuously come in he will tire of it and begin to rip all the tickets at once. When that happens, the chances of using this method successfully will greatly increase and it's up to you to find a group and blend in.

Another advantage is how easily you can switch into the "Desperate Emergency Approach." If the ticket taker counts the tickets, or realizes you're not with the group, any desperate emergency story should work to get you into the theater. Usually the ticket taker will be too busy to question whether or not your story is true and will just let you in.

Chicago, Illinois
Degree of Difficulty: 3 ★★★

This theater is located on the lower level of a department store. The escalators lead directly down to the box office. There's a chance that the employee working there may notice you coming down. Once you reach the bottom, go to the pay phones and pretend to make a call. When people begin exiting the theater, use the "In Thru The Out Door" method. The exit doors by the pay phones lead into the bathroom area. Once in, blending in with the crowds should be no problem.

Disadvantages/Problems You Might Encounter

The disadvantages and problems you might encounter are very similar when using this method. The most common problem occurs when members of the group or family notice you trying to blend in. After the tickets have been ripped and the group is entering the theater, the leader (person with the tickets) may notice you and say to the ticket taker, "He's not with us." Pretend you didn't hear that and quickly switch into the "Desperate Emergency Approach."

This method depends greatly on the ticket taker not counting the tickets, and finding a group to blend in with. If either one does not occur, it would be best to try using one of the other methods to sneak in.

Advice

Only use this method if you are sure it can be done successfully. This is a true challenge and the chances of being caught are great. It works, but only on occasion.

When the tickets have been ripped and the group is entering the theater, never look at the ticket taker as you pass by. Always try to look at the concession stand, or the auditorium playing the movie you came to see, or even pretend that you're listening to a conversation that is taking place in the group. The slightest eye contact with the ticket taker could raise his suspicions and give away your whole plan.

The sooner you find a group to blend in with, the better are your chances of sneaking in. If you find a group right away, it will appear that you were with them the whole time. Standing around by yourself for longer than ten minutes may begin to look a bit suspicious and decrease your chances of blending in with a group inconspicuously.

Recently, I was walking down Hollywood Boulevard and noticed that one of the theaters was having a premier of an eagerly awaited movie. I thought it might be a fun challenge to try to sneak into it. The front was packed with photographers, reporters, and fans hoping to see celebrities. Within minutes, I discovered that a select group of non-celebrities was also attending the screening. These people had the good fortune of winning passes from a local radio station.

They were picking up their passes from the box office and entering the theater through a side door. At this door were two employees, one at each side of the doorway. I noticed that neither of the employees were counting the tickets when the groups approached them. I waited for the moment when both employees were busy, then I squeezed past the groups and entered the theater. One of the employees saw me. I looked at him and mouthed the words, "I'm with them," and pointed to the group with the other ticket taker. The employee smiled and said, "Oh, okay," and turned to rip more tickets. Getting into that premier was definitely one of the high points of my sneaking-in career.

RECAP OF STEPS TO A SUCCESSFUL SNEAK-IN

1. Check the local newspaper movie listings for the theater that is playing the greatest number of movies you would like to see.
2. Call the theater and double check the start times.
3. Call the "for more information" number to find out the running times.
4. Make a schedule.
5. Arrive at the theater and use one of the sneaking-in methods or a variation to get inside.
6. Remember, the bathroom is the safest place to be. Always use it to your advantage.
7. Metamorphosis. A little change will turn you into a whole new person.
8. Blend in with the crowds that are heading to the auditorium that is showing the movie you came to see.

9. Find a prop, such as popcorn, a drink, or any free reading material (Movie Facts, Preview, etc.), to create the impression that you have just arrived at the theater.
10. Enter the auditorium that is playing the first movie on your list. Find a seat and eat, read or pretend to be asleep.
11. When the lights go down, relax and enjoy the movie.
12. When the movie ends, exit one of the back doors, or watch the credits and repeat steps 6 through 11.

Los Angeles, California
Degree of Difficulty: 5 ★★★★★ (Main Auditorium)
2 ★★ (Side Auditoriums)

The most famous theater in the world. You might assume that because of the theater's popularity it would be the most difficult to sneak into, but it's not. There are three auditoriums at this theater. The main auditorium, the one by the celebrity footprints, is the most difficult to sneak into. The other two are simple. Approach the ticket taker at the entrance of the two side auditoriums and tell him the employee at the other door said you could use the bathroom. There actually is a way to get from this side to the main auditorium. When you enter look to your left; there will be a staircase that leads to a door. On the other side of this door is the lobby to the main auditorium. It's tough to get through it without an employee noticing. But, if you see a chance and no one is looking, then it's worth a try.

HOW TO SNEAK IN WITH MORE THAN ONE PERSON

There are many ways to sneak in with more than one person. Some of the most successful ways are done by combining one or more of the "Sneaking In" methods. The more the methods are combined, the greater the amount of people you will be able to sneak in.

One of the most important things to remember when sneaking in with others is to avoid overusing any one method. For instance, if one person sneaks in using the "Desperate Emergency Approach," then another should use "In Thru The Out Door." Too many people approaching a ticket taker within minutes of each other with desperate emergencies will seem a little bit suspicious, and the ticket taker may stop letting people in. So try new ideas and take chances; you never know what might actually work. One last note — when sneaking in with others, always live by this rule:

"Whoever gets in, stays in."

If two or more people sneak in successfully, then those people deserve to stay and watch a movie. Everyone else should pay for a ticket or go to the mall.

The following are examples of the most commonly used methods for sneaking in more than one person. Try them or use parts of each to invent new methods of your own. Remember, creativity is the key to sneaking in successfully.

The Community Ticket

The community ticket is the one ticket that everyone in the group pitches in money to buy. Of course, the amount each person contributes will be considerably less depending upon the number of people in the group and the time of day the ticket is purchased. Now, the first thing the group must do is choose someone to buy the ticket. The person chosen should be the one who is most familiar with the theater and can blend in with the crowds the best. While that person is buying the ticket, the rest of the group will proceed to the predetermined exit doors and wait for them to be opened. Remember, no more than two people should ever stand next to an exit at one time. More than two people will:

1. attract unwanted attention to the group
2. slow down the entrance of the group after the doors have been opened.

Those are the two main reasons groups are caught when trying to sneak in. Many times, the entire group will wait at one door instead of separating to the many other exit doors. The problem with that is that large groups are extremely noticeable. Usually someone on his way to pay for a ticket will notice the group and inform an employee. The employee will then go to that door and open it. The group waiting outside will assume that the door is being opened by the person with the ticket and rush to enter the theater. As they enter, the employee stops them and all plans are ruined.

If things are going as planned, the person with the ticket will enter the theater and go directly to the auditorium that is showing the movie the group came to see. After a few minutes pass, that person will leave the auditorium and walk toward the exit doors. When he is certain that there are no employees in sight, he will push open the doors and walk back to the auditorium. The group waiting outside will quickly enter the theater and head into the first dark auditorium they see. Entering a dark auditorium will offer many advantages, such as:

1. It will be easier to blend in and pass some time without being noticed.
2. It will be nearly impossible for an employee to locate anyone while the auditorium is dark.
3. The movie playing may have begun only a few minutes before. If you find that leaving the auditorium will only result in being caught, remain seated and watch the movie. Hopefully it will be something you would like to see.

Once inside the dark auditorium, immediately find seats, preferably away from each other, relax and watch the movie showing. One common mistake people make is to continuously move around inside the auditorium. Remember, if a movie is already in progress, the people watching the film will be settled in their seats and involved in the plot. There is always the chance that an employee has caught a glimpse of the group rushing into the dark auditorium. If so, the employee will walk into the auditorium in an attempt to find them. The employee will stand at the back of the auditorium for a few minutes, looking for any clues to the whereabouts of the group. If the group is settled in their seats, it will be extremely difficult for an employee to find them.

Five or ten minutes will pass before the employee will decide to walk out. The group should never leave the dark auditorium immediately after the employee has left. The employee may be trying to pull an "Employee Trick." Instead of standing at the back of the auditorium, he will wait outside of it and catch the group as they walk out. When the employee leaves the auditorium, remain seated for a few minutes. After some time has passed, one person from the group will leave the auditorium and proceed directly into the bathroom. In the bathroom the necessary changes will take place, then he will blend in with the crowds and walk to the auditorium where the person with the ticket is waiting. A few minutes later the next person will do the same. The group should never exit the dark auditorium together for several reasons:

1. It's easier to blend in with the crowds by yourself.
2. If an employee did see the group sneak in, he will be looking for a group, not an individual.
3. If the first person that leaves the auditorium is stopped by an employee, the second person will be able to walk past without being noticed and inform the person with the ticket what has happened.

When everyone in the group is finally together in the same auditorium, it is always a good idea to find seats away from each other until the lights go down. This will only be necessary if there are very few people in the auditorium. Sitting away from each other is a safety precaution in case anyone in the group has been followed by an employee; this way the rest of the group will still be safe. If the auditorium is packed, the group could join together, find seats, and enjoy the movie.

Chicago, Illinois
Degree of Difficulty: 2 ★★

This theater has four auditoriums located on the ground level and one upstairs by the bathrooms. All sneaking-in methods work here. Plus, since the bathrooms are on the second level, your chances of success are greatly increased. Many times this theater will show the same movie on more than one screen. This will limit your choice of movies, but other than that it's a cool theater.

Instead of buying a community ticket, someone in the group could use the "Desperate Emergency Approach" to get in and still successfully sneak in others. But actually having a ticket stub will always increase the group's confidence and offer a bit of security once they are inside the theater. If a member of the group has to leave the auditorium for any reason, the ticket stub will be handed to that person just in case an employee happens to approach him.

When using the "Community Ticket" method, quite often the only person who will be able to make it into the theater will be the person with the ticket. That person should always wait in the auditorium until the movie begins. If no one from the group has joined him, he should then leave the auditorium and refund the ticket. The person with the ticket should never stay and watch the movie if the rest of the group was unable to sneak in, unless he really wants to tick the group off.

There is only one additional thing to be aware of when opening exit doors. It is a little-known fact that many theaters have alarm systems connected to the doors. Each time an exit door is opened, the alarm system will be activated. Usually the system is located in an area where a majority of the employees work or pass by on a regular basis, such as the concession stand. Some alarm systems will be box-shaped and exhibit many numbered lights, each one representing a different door. Every time a door is opened, the corresponding light will come on, accompanied by a loud ringing noise. When that happens, the employee nearest the alarm will check to see which door has been opened.

Many times, if the alarm is activated within minutes of a movie's ending time, the employee will assume that people are beginning to leave the theater and will not rush to check on it. But if the alarm goes off when nothing is near an ending time, an employee will immediately be sent to check on the door. This is the reason why it is so important to have two people at the most waiting at each door. The goal is to get the group inside the theater and into a dark auditorium before any employees are sent to check on the door. Two people can enter the theater more quickly than a large group. It's these small challenges that make sneaking in worth it.

The Ticket Stub Hand-Off

"The Ticket Stub Hand-Off" is a good method to use when sneaking in with only one other person. Of course, it may be combined with other methods to sneak in a greater amount of people, but to achieve the greatest success it is best with only one person. This method is most effective when there are two ticket takers and both are constantly busy. It is slightly more challenging when there is only one ticket taker, but it can still be done.

First, like the "Community Ticket" method, each person will pitch in money to buy a ticket. One person will then buy the ticket and enter the theater. The other person will wait at the car or anywhere that is beyond employee viewing distance. The first person will enter the theater and give the ticket to the ticket taker to rip it. When the stub is returned, he will put it in his pocket, get a good look at the ticket takers, and walk in looking for the auditorium showing the movie for which the ticket was bought. After about five or ten minutes, that person will leave the auditorium, return to the same ticket taker and say, "Listen, I have to run to my car for a second. I seem to have misplaced my stub. I just want to be sure I can get back in. I'll be right back." When the ticket taker gives the "okay," the person with the stub will leave the theater and proceed directly to the location where the other person is waiting. At this point the "Ticket Stub Hand-Off" takes place. The ticket stub will now be handed off to the person waiting, along with a brief description of the ticket takers and advice on which one to avoid.

This method is most successful when each person approaches a different ticket taker when entering the theater. The person who originally had the ticket stub will now walk back to the same ticket taker that let him leave, and reenter the theater. When the other person notices a large crowd beginning to form around the employees, he should enter the theater, approach the other ticket taker and say, "I was already in. I just had to run to my car for a second."

The ticket taker will look at the stub, notice that it is for a movie that is starting soon, and let the person inside. That person will then walk to the auditorium and find a seat. Once again, it is best not to sit together until the lights go down. There's always the chance that one of the ticket takers may walk through the auditorium, see the two of you together, realize what has happened and put an end to your plans. When the lights go down, join together, and relax.

Los Angeles, California
Degree of Difficulty: 5 ★★★★★

Quite possibly the toughest theater in Los Angeles to sneak into. The box office is on the ground level of a mall. To enter the theater you must take the escalators which lead directly to the ticket takers. There are almost always more than one employee taking tickets. Plus, there are more employees near the front who are checking in the people with "advance ticket" credit card orders. Another problem is that there is almost always an employee checking ticket stubs in front of each different auditorium. This theater is a true challenge.

HOW TO SNEAK IN WITH A DATE WITHOUT HER THINKING YOU'RE CHEAP

As the title suggests, this is a strictly "Guys Only" chapter. So, if you are female, kindly skip over this chapter and begin reading "What Happens And What To Do When Caught." Thank you.

When planning to sneak in with a date, you must remember two important things:

1. Women hate cheap guys. You can never let a woman think you're cheap, even though you are.
2. Women love guys who live on the edge. Guys who are adventurous. Guys who don't follow society's rules. Rebels.

In order to avoid looking cheap you must always remember one thing: the idea of sneaking into the movies must come from her. You, the guy, can never suggest sneaking in. You can put the idea into her head, but you can never say, "Hey, let's sneak into a movie tonight." How to go about putting the idea into her head and having her suggest sneaking in will depend primarily upon how smoothly you handle the situation. The following is an example of how to get her to suggest the idea. Of course, the conversation will not go exactly like this, but this example will give you a general idea of what should happen.

The evening will probably begin with you and your date (or girlfriend) sitting around trying to find something to do. Eventually the idea of going to the movies will be brought up. You will both start looking through the movie listings, discussing the movies you would like to see. You notice that many of the movies that have been mentioned are playing at a theater that is easy to sneak into. You then say, "Wow, most of the movies we want to see are playing at the Esquire. I haven't seen a movie there since I sneaked in and saw..."

This will be the first and only time you ever bring up the idea of sneaking in. The rest will depend on her. If she has any interest in what you just said, her response should be, "What do you mean, since you 'sneaked in' there?"

If she shows no interest in what you have said, then the chances are implanting the idea of sneaking in into her head is going to be considerably more difficult. Let's suppose her response was positive. You then tell her, "Oh, that theater is easy to sneak into. I do it all the time." When you say this, be sure to act a little overconfident and cocky. Women love that. She will find you and the idea of sneaking in a bit more interesting. She may then say, "But how do you get in?"

If she says anything along those lines, you can assume that the possibility of sneaking in is beginning to tempt her. Now is the crucial part. You must convince her that sneaking in is easy. If you say anything slightly negative, your whole plan will be ruined. Say something like: "It's easy. There are hundreds of ways to get inside. But the best time to do it is when the theater is packed." If the conversation is taking place on a Friday or Saturday night, follow up with: "Like tonight would be a perfect night to do it. There are going to be a lot of people there, especially with all these new movies opening." That should be all you need to say. You never want to push the idea of sneaking in too hard, just enough to make her seriously consider it. At this point, she may say something like, "But what happens if you're caught?"

This is the time to wipe any remaining doubt out of her mind. With confidence and pride say, "I've never been caught sneaking into this theater. It's too easy to get in there." Don't say anything more. Let her think about it for a few minutes. After some thought, she will begin to see the humor in sneaking in. Then, with a rush of excitement, as if she just came up with this great idea, she will say, "Let's sneak into a movie tonight!" Don't get excited. Stay calm and say, "Well, I don't know. Do you really think we should try it?" If she replies with anything like, "Sure, why not? It's worth a try. It will be fun," then you know your plan has worked. Now you should say something like, "All right, but I can't promise we'll get in. I guess you're right, it is worth a try." This will reinforce that sneaking in was her idea and that you're only doing it because she wants to.

After you have protected yourself from looking cheap, it's now time to show her that you're a guy who likes to live on the edge, a guy who is adventurous, a guy who lives by his own rules, a rebel. Before attempting to sneak in with a date, it is very important that you take control of the situation. Women love it when guys take control. Take a few minutes and let her know:

1. How you plan to sneak her in
2. That she must stay as close to you as possible at all times
3. That she must always play along with any story you give to an employee if a problem arises.

This way she will know what to expect and can help out if needed. And, most importantly, ALWAYS STAY WITH YOUR DATE. Never leave her alone waiting at an exit door or make her do something by herself. Do everything as a couple. This will impress her.

HOLLYWOOD, CALIFORNIA
Degree of Difficulty: 3 ★★★

This is the nicest theater in Hollywood to sneak into. On weekends, there is always a crowd. The best method to use is the "In Thru The Out Door." Once you have made it inside, walk directly up the stairs to the bathroom near the balcony. Then, blend in with the crowds and find a seat in the balcony area. The theater is so big that once you're inside the chances of being caught are slim. If you plan to sneak in with a date, this is a nice theater to choose.

The best method to use when sneaking in with a date is "In Thru The Out Door." Only this time, instead of sneaking in using the back doors, the best doors to use will be the ones in the front of the theater. Wait until a movie has ended and people are beginning to exit the theater. When you notice that the employees are busy, you and your date should push your way though the crowd and enter the theater.

Once inside, go directly to the concession stand and wait in line. Nothing looks more natural at a movie theater than a couple waiting in line to buy refreshments. And after all, since you didn't pay for her ticket, you should at least buy her something to eat.

After you have bought her something to eat, enter the auditorium showing the movie you came to see, find a seat and relax. If the employees are still cleaning the auditorium, just hang out in the lobby with the other couples. The theater employees will never question a couple waiting around the lobby with some popcorn. If an employee does see you and your date entering through the exit doors, just say "She left her purse inside. We just came out of (name a movie that just ended)." Since the majority of theater employees are guys, they know never to challenge a woman when she says she has lost something. So enter the theater, blend in with the crowds, and go to the auditorium showing the movie you came to see.

Don't feel bad if you and your date are caught and escorted out of the theater. Remember, it was her idea to try sneaking in in the first place. But if you do sneak in successfully, LOOK OUT. Women love to sneak in and will quickly become hooked on it. It will become an obsession, almost like a drug. They will beg to do it all the time and will become angry when you tell them it's not a good time or you're not in the mood. Be Warned!

WHAT HAPPENS AND WHAT TO DO WHEN CAUGHT

The fear of being caught is the Number One reason most people never try sneaking into the movies. People imagine that they will be arrested, thrown in jail, and stuck with a criminal record for the rest of their lives. However, according to one Los Angeles police officer: "Sneaking into the movies is against the law and is a form of trespassing, but no one is going to go to jail for it." So, with that in mind, the fear of sneaking in should be eliminated and it's up to you to take the chance.

If a person is caught, usually the worst thing that will happen is that he will be escorted out of the theater by an employee. Occasionally a policeman or security guard will be called in to handle the situation. But that will usually only happen if the person caught becomes rude, loud, or obnoxious. If you are caught, it is very important never to put up a fight. Putting up a fight or arguing with an employee could:

1. Bring unwanted attention to yourself. Remember, the key to sneaking in is to keep a low profile.
2. Create a bad situation that could get you in serious trouble.
3. Make it easier for the employees to remember you and decrease any chances of sneaking into that theater in the future.

The risk of being caught, that element of danger, is what makes sneaking in successfully such a thrill. Never feel bad about being caught; it's all part of the game. Always leave with your self-respect and confidence intact, knowing that the next time you attempt sneaking in at this theater they won't catch you. There's nothing better than sneaking into a theater at which you have previously been caught.

Los Angeles, California
Degree of Difficulty: 4 ★★★★

This theater is not even worth your time. Not because it's difficult, but because you are forced to spend money before you even arrive at the theater. This theater is located at one end of an outdoor mall. To reach the mall, you must pay to park your car in one of the parking structures. The price is always subject to change, but will be no less than six dollars. The best way to avoid the parking fee is to park your car elsewhere and walk up the hill to the mall. If you do go to see a movie there, "Pay For One, Stay For More" works fine. But it's always best to go somewhere else and sneak in without paying.

The following is an example of what happens and what you should do if you're caught:

You have already used one of the sneaking-in methods to get into the theater and are now sitting in an auditorium pretending to be asleep. You begin sensing that there are people approaching your seat. Suddenly, you feel a tap on your shoulder and hear someone say, "Excuse me, sir?"

Slowly open your eyes. Remember, you're "in the moment" — someone is rudely waking you from a sleep. Sometimes, the person that is waking you may just be someone wanting to get past you into the aisle, but most of the time it will be an employee. If it is an employee, stay calm and find out what he wants. There is always the chance that you may not be caught. Now, turn to the employees standing in front of you and get a good look at them. This is the only time you will actually look at them face to face. There will usually be two or more employees standing in front of you. When it comes to throwing people out, theater employees will always travel in groups. The reason: theater employees are wimps. What probably happened was that one employee saw you sneak in. He then became nervous and went and told some other employees what he saw. Those employees then pretended to be tough, and said, "Let's go throw that guy out!"

So now you have these wimpy theater employees standing in front of you (pretending to be tough, hoping some girls will notice), with the intent to "throw you out." The ironic thing about this whole situation is that you are still in control. Quite often, only one employee actually saw you sneak in; the rest are taking his word for it. The employees realize that the only way to prove that someone has sneaked in is to find out if they have a ticket stub. So until they prove you don't have one, you're still in control. One of the employees will then say, "Excuse me, sir, but could we please see your ticket stub?"

Don't forget, you're "in the moment." You just woke up and are still a bit confused. Say something like, "My ticket stub?" then begin to go through your pockets slowly. The more slowly you look for the ticket stub, the more it will seem like you really might have one. This will make the employee who saw you sneak in a little nervous. To his relief, you finally give up the search and say, "Oh, man, I can't seem to find it."

Always try to keep your voice soft and mellow. You don't want to attract the attention of the other people in the auditorium. At this point, the employees know you have sneaked in, and you know they know. The "toughest" employee will say, "I'm sorry, sir, but I'm going to have to ask you to leave the theater."

Now casually begin gathering up your things. When you're ready to leave, stand up and start walking towards the exit doors inside the auditorium. Always try to avoid being escorted out the front doors of the theater. Your goal is to exit the theater quickly and with very few people (other employees, people who paid for a ticket) noticing. If the employees do escort you towards the front doors, walk a few steps ahead of them. This way it will appear that you're leaving the theater on your own.

Always remember to wait a few weeks before returning to a theater at which you have been caught. That should be plenty of time for the employees to forget about you. There are thousands of movie theaters; if you're caught at one, go and try at another.

It's best to go where there are many theaters within walking distance of each other, such as on Hollywood Boulevard. For example, if you are caught at one theater, just walk across the street to another and try to sneak in there. If that fails, try the next one. If you keep trying, there's no reason you shouldn't be able to sneak into a movie by the end of the night. But, if you find that you're continuously being caught, maybe it's time to give up sneaking-in altogether and just stick with the many other ways to beat the high cost of movie tickets.

OTHER WAYS TO BEAT THE HIGH COST OF MOVIE TICKETS

Matinees And Twilight Screenings

Since the majority of people go to the movies at night, most theaters offer special discounted tickets during the slow hours of the day and try to bring in more business. The most common discounted ticket is the matinee. Matinees are usually the first showing of the day, and the cost of the ticket is approximately one-third off the regular admission price. Some theaters will offer the matinee ticket price for any showing that begins before six p.m.

Other theaters, instead of extending the matinee price until six, will have an additional discounted showing called a "Twilight Screening." The twilight screening is usually one dollar cheaper than the matinee and is offered for any movie that begins between four and six p.m. Each film playing at the theater will have one screening during that time. So, if you are actually going to pay for a ticket, going to the movies during either of these screening times will be your best bet.

Advantages

There are many advantages to the matinee and twilight screenings. The greatest advantage, of course, is that you don't pay full price. You will see first-run movies in a nice theater and pay a reasonable price.

If you attend a matinee or twilight screening on a weekday, you will notice that the theater is not very crowded. That alone has many advantages, such as:

1. You will not have to wait in lines at the box office or the concession stand
2. You will always be able to find a good seat
3. You may possibly be the only person in the auditorium.

There's nothing better than going to the movies with a group of friends and discovering you have the entire auditorium to yourselves; it will feel like you're at someone's house watching a movie on a big screen in their living room. This is the only time when you can be as loud as you want in a theater without people complaining. Remember, the louder you get, the more fun you have.

Another advantage to the matinee and twilight screenings is that the films end early in the day. This will offer you the opportunity to use the "Pay For One, Stay For More" method to sneak into more movies. But, if you choose not to stay, you have at least seen one movie at a discounted price. Plus, it's a great feeling to leave a theater when the sun is still out. Quite often, your mood for the rest of the day will be determined by the movie experience.

Chicago, Illinois
Degree of Difficulty: 5 (Section in mall) ★★★★★
4 (Section outside mall) ★★★★

This is the most difficult theater in Chicago to sneak into. The theater is divided into two sections. One is located inside the mall on the second floor; the other is outside the mall at ground level. To my knowledge, there is no way to sneak from one level to the next. The entrance to the section inside the mall is small. The box office is located between two sets of doors. The ticket taker is always stationed at one of these doorways, but the other one will only be used when people exit the theater. When a movie ends and people begin to leave, another employee will be sent to guard those doors. The section outside the mall is slightly easier to sneak into, but the lobby is about as far as you will get. The auditoriums are lined up next to each other and roped off so that the only way to enter any auditorium is to pass an employee who will be checking all ticket stubs before letting anyone in. There are many theaters within walking distance of each other in Chicago. The best advice is to go somewhere else to try to sneak in.

Disadvantages

Even though matinees and twilight screenings are great, they both have a few disadvantages. The main disadvantage is that some theaters offer only the first showing of the day at the matinee price. Quite often, the only showing is between twelve and two o'clock in the afternoon. With a showing so early, many people are unable to take advantage of this low ticket price because they are stuck in school or work. There are a few theaters that will schedule their matinee showing as early as ten or eleven in the morning and not offer any other discounted tickets throughout the day. Always try to avoid going to these theaters, unless you're planning on sneaking in.

The main disadvantage of twilight screenings is that they are very popular. There are many reasons for their popularity:

1. The ticket price is the lowest of the day.
2. The screenings are later in the afternoon which makes it easier for more people to attend.
3. There is only one showing of each movie during the twilight hours.

During the weekdays the crowds are not a problem, but on the weekends these screenings sell out quickly. So be aware that on an opening weekend of an eagerly awaited film, lines for this screening will begin to form early. The best way to avoid waiting in lines and worrying that the movie is going to sell out is to buy your ticket in advance. When you do this, be sure to tell the box office that you want a twilight-screening ticket. This way you won't accidentally be charged the matinee price.

Of course, after you have purchased the ticket, you can use it at any time or even on another day. Most of the time the ticket takers never check the time or date on the ticket before they rip it. If the ticket has a big M or T on it, use it only for a matinee or twilight screening. If you try using it at night, tell the ticket taker that your car wouldn't start or that you were stuck in traffic and couldn't make it to the theater on time.

Second-Run Theaters
(Dollar Houses)

Second-run theaters, better known as dollar houses, are quite often the last opportunity for you to see a semi-current release at a theater. After a movie has lost first-run appeal, either because everyone has seen it or because it was so bad that no one wants to see it, the second-run theaters will acquire it. This way the studios still can make a little money at the box office before the film is released on video. You can usually find the second-run theaters under the heading "Independent Theaters" in the movie listings section of your local newspaper.

Advantages

The main advantage to seeing a movie at a second-run theater is the ticket price. The price will vary at the different theaters, but it will always be under three-fifty. Unlike the first-run theaters, which only offer matinee and twilight screenings at a discounted price, the second-run theaters' ticket price will remain the same for any showing at any time of the day. Some dollar houses also offer a matinee ticket price which can be as low as a dollar. You can't beat that.

Another advantage is that most of the dollar houses show double features, so you can see two movies and still pay only one low price. Many dollar houses are also multi-plexes, which offer a wide variety of movies to choose from. With so many movies available, it's easy to create your own double feature. Most of the employees that work at dollar houses seem unconcerned about people's sneaking around to the different movies. Even so, it's still a good idea to sneak around carefully. Every so often you may encounter an employee on a power trip, but for the most part the employees are laid back and will let you get away with it.

One thing that you will notice at dollar houses is that their concession stand will have the best selection of candy. Not that this is a major advantage, it's just something cool. Since the theater is not making much money at the box office, the majority of their income will be generated from the concession stand. The bigger the selection, the more people will buy.

Los Angeles, California
Degree of Difficulty: 4 (Sneaking in without paying) ★★★★
2 (Pay for one, Stay for more) ★★

This theater is located on the second floor of a plaza. The escalators in the front lead directly to the box office. The best method to use is the "Pay For One, Stay For More." Once inside the theater, it's easy to proceed from one movie to the next. The chances of an employee noticing you trying to sneak in using one of the other methods are very great, so it's almost not worth the effort.

Disadvantages

Dollar houses are great, but there are a few things to be aware of if you choose to see movies at them. The first is the atmosphere. Many of the second-run theaters were old movie palaces or neighborhood theaters at one time. When the first-run multi-plex theaters began to open near the malls, the neighborhood theaters couldn't compete. So they either closed down or started showing second-run movies. Since the owners charge such low ticket prices, there is less money available to spend on the maintenance of the theater. As a result, the inside of some theaters are beginning to deteriorate. Some obvious forms of deterioration you may encounter are:

1. A seat or a row of seats may be in need of repair
2. Paint may be peeling or light fixtures may be hanging off the wall
3. The floors may need a good cleaning.

Of course, there are some very nice dollar houses. The really nice dollar houses are the ones that have been completely remodeled specifically for the purpose of showing second-run films. Many times, a theater that had only one big auditorium will be converted into a number of smaller auditoriums. Some of the auditoriums will be tiny and may give you the feeling that you're watching a movie in a box. But the atmosphere is clean and the price is right.

If the theater has not been remodeled, you may still be able to note some of the old splendor the movie palace once possessed and imagine what a great theater it could be again if only some time and money were invested in taking care of it. It sucks when an old theater is demolished; it's like ripping apart history and destroying the past to make room for another parking lot.

Another thing to be aware of is the type of people who go to the dollar houses. The audience will vary according to the location of the theater. If the theater is in a college town, most of the people who attend will be students and locals. If the theater is in a big city, a wide range of different types of people will often use these theaters as a cheap way of getting out of the cold. They usually find a seat in the back and try to catch up on sleep. If you sit far enough away, you won't even know they are there. After you have avoided the homeless, the only problem you may encounter will be the loud obnoxious people who talk all through the movie. For some reason, people think that just because the ticket was so inexpensive, they now have the right to talk all through the film. It's always best to find an aisle seat so you can easily move when they won't shut up.

Production Screenings

A production screening is the showing of a new film to a select target audience before it is released to the general public. The film is presented as a "work in progress;" the studios use these screenings as a way of finding out audience reactions before the film is completed. After the film has ended, the audience is asked to fill out a questionnaire. A few examples of the questions are:

1. What scenes did or didn't you like?
2. What do you think about the different characters and the actors' performance?
3. How would you rate the overall story and plot?
4. Would you recommend this movie to a friend?

The studio will review the questionnaires and note some of the common responses. Then, according to popular opinion, they will make the appropriate changes.

The only way to attend a production screening is to have a pass. Passes are easy to obtain. The best place to get a pass is at any popular first-run theater. Usually, a production screening "recruiter" will be standing in front of the theater, asking people if they would like to see a free movie. Approach that person and tell him you would like to go. Before giving you the pass he will ask your age, your occupation, and whether or not you have been to a production screening within the past three months. The recruiter is required to ask these questions to insure that you qualify for the target market of the movie and that you do not work for the entertainment business. People who work in the entertainment business are prohibited from attending these screenings. There are many explanations for this and according to one market research department, "We're not allowed to discuss the reasons — they just can't go." So, when they ask those questions, give a fake name, say you're a waiter, and tell them you have never been to a screening. It's possible to see two or more screenings per week.

Advantages

There are many advantages to production screenings. One major advantage is that the movie is free. If it turns out to be a bad movie, so what? It was free. Everything is better when it's free, even movies that suck. However, if the movie is great, then you have just previewed an eagerly-awaited film months before it will be released to the general public. Plus, you have seen a version of the film that may or may not be the same that the public will see when it is released.

Another advantage is that these screenings are probably the only time when you can give your opinion about a movie and the studios will listen. If many people feel the same way as you do about a particular character or scene, the studios will make the changes. Many endings of films have been changed due to the audience responses at those screenings.

The greatest advantage to these screenings is the chance that you may be paid. Many times a discussion group of about twenty people will be held after the screening. These twenty people are selected while waiting in line before the movie begins. The chances of being chosen are slim. The best way to be sure you will be part of that group is to find the member of the marketing research company who is carrying a clipboard and is talking to only a few people waiting in line. Politely call the person over and ask if he is picking people to be part of the discussion group. If he says he is, ask if you can be part of it. Usually they will include you.

After the movie has ended and everyone has left, the twenty people who have been selected will be asked to sit in the front two rows. Then someone will begin asking the group their opinions about the movie. Many times the producers or directors will be sitting in the back, listening to the discussion. Ten minutes later the discussion group will end and each person in the group will be paid approximately ten dollars. Even if you don't say anything, you will still be paid. There's nothing better than being paid to see a movie.

Disadvantages

When attending a production screening, there are a few things you should keep in mind. The first is that the film is a "work in progress." It's a rough cut, quickly edited together to give the studio an idea of how an audience may react and whether the movie has the potential to make money. Before the movie begins, someone from the market research department will remind the audience that the film is a "work in progress" and to be aware that:

1. Black lines or scratches may appear on the film.
2. The credits and titles may be omitted.
3. A scene or shot may be missing.
4. Some scenes may have color problems
5. Some of the special effects may not be added.
6. All the music is temporary.

These are just a few of the problems the film may have. Now you can understand why it's free.

Another disadvantage is that seating is never guaranteed; it is on a first-come, first-served basis. Hundreds of these passes are handed out each day. So in order to be sure that you will get a seat, you must arrive at the theater or studio (wherever the screening is taking place) about forty-five minutes to an hour earlier than the time printed on the pass. Even that early, there will be people already lining up. Then you will have to wait over an hour before they start to let people inside. The wait seems long, but it's the only way to be sure to get a seat. Always keep in mind: it's free.

Renting A Video

Because the price of movie tickets continually increases, many people are choosing to remain in the comfort of their own homes renting videos instead. Renting a video is a great way to beat the high cost of movie tickets. Most neighborhood video stores charge under two dollars for a one-night rental, which is a good deal. Some of the larger video chains will charge over three dollars but will rent you the movie for two nights. Usually, the movies are watched the same night they are rented, then returned the next day. So people end up paying more for nothing. Only rent from the larger chains after you have first checked the neighborhood video stores for the movie you want to see or the hard-to-find films.

Advantages

Renting a video has many advantages. The first is the price. If you split the rental fee with a few friends, renting can be a fun, inexpensive way to spend an evening. Plus, with the money you save, you can buy pizza and beer.

Another advantage is that you can enjoy the movie in the comfort of your own home, at your convenience. You don't have to worry about getting to the theater on time or trying to find a parking space. With a video, you can rewind scenes you like and watch them again, pause the tape when you get hungry, or watch half the movie and save the rest for later. These options will usually become necessities when you rent a video with your girlfriend or date. It's a proven fact that it is nearly impossible to watch a whole video with a date without having to stop it at least once. Any time the plot begins to slow down and become boring, the touchy-feely games will start and the movie will be stopped. Most of the time the video will be returned without ever being completely watched.

Finally, you won't have to deal with the long lines at the concession stand and be overcharged for your food. For the price of some popcorn, a drink and candy, you can stay home and order Chinese food or a pizza.

Disadvantages

The biggest disadvantage to renting a video is that you lose the "movie experience." All films, except for the made-for-TV or direct-to-video movies, are meant to be seen on a big screen in a theater. The studios spend millions of dollars on different effects (lighting, sound, etc.) to create a true movie experience. When the movies are transferred to video, many of these effects are lost. The small-screen stereo sound of a television cannot compare to the big-screen digital Dolby surround-sound of a theater.

When some movies are transferred to video, the format of the film is completely changed to fit onto a television screen. This is most noticeable when a film was originally made in Cinemascope. Cinemascope is a wide-screen format; when that is transferred to video the results are usually disastrous. The two most common ways to transfer Cinemascope to video are:

1. Squeezing the picture together to fit onto the screen. This will cause the whole image to look thin and stretched out, or

2. Chopping off the ends of the picture. This is extremely noticeable when you can only see half of the person's face on the screen.

Once you are aware of these techniques it will become difficult to sit and enjoy a movie which has been transferred from Cinemascope to video. The best way to see Cinemascope movies on video is to rent the letter-box format. Many people dislike letter-box formats because of the distracting black spaces at the top and bottom of the screen. The black is there to help create the original wide-screen Cinemascope effect. Even though the whole picture does appear on the screen, it still can never compare to the big screen of the theater.

Another disadvantage is the hassle of going to the video store and searching for a movie you want to see. There's always the chance that the movie you really want to see will already be rented. Then you end up spending the next thirty minutes trying to find another movie, become frustrated, and just grab something you really don't want to see. But because you've wasted so much time at the video store, you feel obligated to rent something. By the time you get home it's late. So you decide to wait and watch it the next day. Then, after you finally watch it and try to return it, the video store is closed. So you're charged a late fee and it ends up costing you as much as it would have if you paid to see the movie at a theater. Other than that, renting a video is a great way to beat the high cost of movie tickets.

Zion, Illinois
Degree of difficulty: 1 ★

Nice little small town theater. The best way to get in is:
1. if you are female, ask to see the manager, Dave. Flirt with him. If he thinks you like him, he will let you in for free.
2. if you are male, just say you know me and that I said he would let you in.

YOU WILL ALSO WANT TO READ: